Illustration by Dr. Larry Peterson

Puppy Talk

Conversations Between Grandpa and His Son's Puppy –
Remi

Authored by Jeff Kallis
May 17, 2022

Remi was born on February 4, 2021, with a litter of seven. She is a F2B generation mini-goldendoodle. Her papa, Henry, is an F1 (1st generation mini-goldendoodle backcross). Her mama is Geneva, an F1B (1st generation mini-goldendoodle). Remi has a higher percentage of golden retriever in her gene pool.

Our son, Caleb, named Remi after the dog in the television series, Heartland. The character Amy Fleming has a dog named Remi in real life that also appeared in the show during a few episodes. Caleb loves the show so much he named Remi after her.

Words of Caution: This book is not to be read with a mouthful of any beverage, or while driving.

Remi

May 15, 2022 (15 months old)

Copyright © 2022 Jeff Kallis

All rights reserved.

Table of Contents

Artwork by AnnaliseArt, Pixabay.com

There's a first time for everything. Puppies are no different than humans in that regard. Seeing the world through a child's eyes for the first time is a great refresher course for those of us who are older in the tooth. Things we take for granted or don't appreciate like we once did. The same can be said for our 4-legged friends.

Every noise or object is a new discovery:

- The funny noise that a plastic grocery bag makes when it is set on the floor. And there is something in it.

- A sock can provide hours of enjoyment. Best of all it is silent and can be stored away for play time later.

- Watching movement on a television, particularly when something familiar barks at you. Who cannot help but laugh at the little pup trying desperately to crawl into the television screen or search behind it to find their new-found friend?

- Of course, seeing one's own reflection in a mirror for the first time and not realizing the cute little creature staring back at them is none other than themselves is a sight to behold. The mimicking of their every move can be a bit unnerving for a little puppy. Like some humans, a puppy can be fascinated with looking at themselves.

- Watching paper spit out of a printer is fascinating for a puppy as well. It moves, makes a noise and then it stops. What puppy wouldn't want to bark at it, lunge at it, take a bite out of it, or run away with it.

- Whether it's a blade of grass, a leaf blowing in the wind, or a bird flying high above, a little puppy can provide you with hours of entertainment. Not to mention, questions.

- During one of Remi's first experiences with chasing a bird and a bumble bee, she confided in me later that Grandma and I were right. The birds and the bees are a lot of fun but it's exhausting.

Just like with a newborn child experiencing their long list of "firsts", it's a great reminder to stop and appreciate all the things that we take for granted. But to the little one's it's a whole new world. With lots of questions, and barks.

Artwork by OpenClipart-Vectors, Pixabay.com

Just like with a child, potty training a little puppy takes a lot of patience and stain remover. It didn't take long before Remi realized she was being treated differently in this regard. We had to have a sit down to smooth this over.

On one occasion, Grandpa had to have a discussion with Remi after she went potty inside.

Grandpa:
"Remi, that's a No-No. You need to potty outside."

Remi:
"Grandpa, why do I always have to go outside to go potty? You never do. Except for that one time we went into the woods in a hurry."

Grandpa:
"Well, Remi, it took me years of training to get this right. Grandma still tells me I forgot to lift the seat or missed the target altogether. Let's just give you free rein to go wherever you want to go outside. Look at the bright side, you never have to clean up after yourself."

Remi:
"Thank you, Grandpa. I step in it enough; I don't need that too. And I promise I won't take Grandma to that spot."

Grandpa:
"Sure. I know how you feel about keeping secrets from Grandma. There's a pup cup in it for you if you keep it between us. Otherwise, say goodbye to the drive-thrus for you."

Sitting around a campfire.

Sometimes the best conversations happen around a campfire. There's something about the peaceful nature of a glowing flame that opens a person's soul, sharing things they otherwise wouldn't.

Remi was having trouble with a neighbor dog. After one of Remi's neighbors walked by and barked at her, Remi was not having any of it.

Remi:
"He wasn't very nice to me, Grandpa. I can't even repeat what he said. I'll show him a thing or two. Speaking of #2, I have a good idea where I can do it."

Grandpa:
"Now, Remi. You need to be a good neighbor. Besides, you don't know where he lives."

Remi:
"Grandpa, I can track him down. One good sniff and I can find him anywhere."

Random questions as the fire flickers:

Remi:
"Grandpa, when do I get my own closet for clothes like you and Grandma?"

Grandpa:
"I can barely fit my clothes in the closet, Remi. Your Grandma needs a lot of space. How about we get you a little tub? Besides, it cost us a fortune to add on to the house for all your toys."

Speaking of hot air:

Remi:
"Grandpa, if you think it's bad when you break wind, imagine how I feel. I can smell it from a mile away. When I'm sitting on your lap, that's just rude. It burns my nose and makes me sneeze."

Grandpa:
"When you're older, you'll understand."

Remi:
"Grandpa, why do I have to go to my kennel when you leave the house?"

Grandpa:
"It's for your own good, Remi. It keeps you safe and out of mischief."

Remi:
"Where do you go without me anyway?"

Grandpa:
"There are lots of places we go when we put you in your kennel. We go to church, a restaurant, to a store, a movie, or to visit friends and family."

Remi:

"I like all those things Grandpa. I really like it when you and Caleb take me to Home Depot. I get to see other dogs there too. And the people who wear the vests are always so nice to me.

There are tunnels for me to walk through. So many things are at eye level that I don't even need to stand on my back legs to see. Some shelves even have treats. You always take me with you when you go to that house don't you, Grandpa?"

Grandpa:

"Sometimes I have to go there alone."

Remi:

"Why do you have to do that, Grandpa?"

Grandpa:

"Well, sometimes I really need to concentrate to make sure I get the right thing."

Remi:

"I can help you find things, Grandpa. I'm very good at finding stuff. They're hiding a lot of things on those shelves."

Grandpa:

"Good point. I'll try to keep that in mind."

Remi:

"Grandpa, why don't I ever get to go inside a restaurant?"

Grandpa:

"Restaurants are for humans to sit down and eat together. Sometimes we can take you when the restaurant lets pets eat outside on the patio. Like the Purple Goat. Otherwise, customers want to have a clean environment. And some people are allergic to animals."

Remi:

"Some people are allergic to me, Grandpa?"

Grandpa:

"Hard to believe, isn't it, someone as adorable as you."

Remi:
"I've never seen a purple goat, Grandpa. Have you?

Grandpa:
"I haven't, Remi. But I have seen the greatest <u>of</u> <u>all</u> <u>t</u>ime, Tom Brady."

Remi:
"He is the GOAT, Grandpa. But he needs to tell the people who catch his throws to return the ball to him. They always run away from him instead. And sometimes the people run out of their yard and jump up into a stranger's lap. You're never happy when I do that to you, Grandpa."

Grandpa:
"Good call, Remi. Good call."

Remi still wasn't sure about the purple part:

Remi:
"Grandpa, Tom Brady isn't purple. So why do they call it a purple goat?

Grandpa:
"That's a different kind of goat, Remi. That's the Minnesota Vikings."

Remi:
"Why are they called that, Grandpa?"

Grandpa:
"It's because they have never won a super bowl, Remi."

Remi:
"I know how they feel. I'm still waiting for a bowl full of my favorite treats. That would be really super."

Remi is always looking out for what's good for the family:

Remi:
"Grandpa, you and Grandma could save a lot of money on your grocery bill if you let me eat at the restaurants. I don't expect much. I just need one course. You can have the rest."

Grandpa:

"Speaking of courses, you did a really good job running through the obstacle course at puppy school last week. "

Remi:

"Thank you, Grandpa. Caleb always gives me a treat when I do it right."

Grandpa:

"Well, you're a fast learner."

Remi:

"Thank you, Grandpa. It's hard to concentrate though when there are so many cute boy puppies there. I see them watching me. That's when I really put on a show and prance around. They seem to like that."

Grandpa:

"Remember, Remi. You're there to learn, not put on a show."

Remi:

"I thought I was doing a pretty good job at both, Grandpa."

Sometimes Remi doesn't know what's in her best interest:

Remi:

"Grandpa, why don't you ever sing me to sleep?"

Grandpa:

"I only sing in church, where I know God will forgive me."

Remi:

"Oh. It's for the best then. When you do sing, it makes the hairs on the back of my neck stand straight up. Maybe you can just hum."

Grandpa:

"Thanks for the feedback."

Remi:
"Grandpa, why don't you ever say "Yes" to me like you do to Grandma?"

Grandpa:
"Well, it depends upon the question, or suggestion. There's some things Grandpa never says no to when Grandma asks."

Remi:
"You mean when Grandma asks you to help her clean the house?"

Grandpa:
"Not exactly. But it does involve a lot of energy and I usually take a nap afterward."

Remi:
"You mean when you have to do the dishes?"

Grandpa:
"Not exactly. I think we should go inside and see what Grandma is doing. Maybe she's been working too hard and needs to take a nap."

Remi:
"Oh. Are you going to lock the door again?"

Grandpa:
"Isn't there a rodent out here that you can chase?"

Remi doesn't always understand why Grandpa does certain things:

Remi:
"Grandpa, why do you light a fire to all those sticks that I like to play with?"

Grandpa:
"Because the sticks that I pick up that fall from the trees make good kindling for the fire."

Remi:
"It doesn't seem right that a toy of mine has to go up in smoke."

Sometimes Remi forgets who's who:

Remi:
"Grandpa, why do I always have to get the ball when you tell me to fetch it?"

Grandpa:
"Remi, if you have to ask that question, then the retriever in you isn't so golden."

Remi:
"Grandpa, I'm not just going to lay down and rollover for nothing."

Left: Milo - Toy Poodle
Right: Bella - Siberian Husky

Bella and Milo

These two are our son, Chris, and his girlfriend, Riley's, dogs. Bella is a Siberian husky and Milo is a toy poodle. Bella is a gentle giant. Milo has short-dog syndrome. He's a high-strung "guard dog", protecting his favorite people from everyone else. Or so he thinks.

Remi doesn't always understand the behaviors of her little cousin, Milo. What Milo lacks in size, he makes up for with his ear-piercing bark.

Milo is very protective of Grandpa, even in Remi's house. That doesn't always sit well with Remi.

Both have had to go to the time-out-chair more than once for biting.

Remi:
"Grandpa, Milo barks so loud it hurts my ears. Do your ears ring too?"

Grandpa:
"Yes, but Milo is your cousin. He's very protective. The little ones always have a big bark."

Remi:
"He must have been the runt of the litter."

Grandpa:
"Now, now, Remi. Milo is a toy poodle. He's supposed to be small."

Remi:
"Did you say 'toy' Grandpa? Hmmm."

Remi has grown fond of her older cousin, Bella. She's very tolerant of Remi now that Remi has lost her puppy teeth.

Remi:
"Grandpa, Bella is such a nice friend to me. She lets me grab her around the neck and then she does it to me. Milo never lets me do that to him."

"But sometimes, Bella lifts her front paw and flattens me to the ground. Why does she do that to me?"

Grandpa:
"That means you're pushing her limits. She's telling you to chill out."

Remi:
"Oh, that's why she does that. Is it kind of like the speed limit that you always ignore?"

Grandpa:
"Remi, once again, you've missed the point. Besides, the posted limit is way too slow. But don't tell Grandma."

Remi:

"Grandpa, I'm just going to do what you do, not what you say."

Grandpa:

"Remi, that's not how this conversation is supposed to go. Go find Caleb or Grandma."

Remi – 15 months old.

Chloe (front) and Colby

Chloe and Colby

Sometimes curiosity isn't just coming from the cat.

Remi:
"Why don't we have a kitten, Grandpa? They look like they would be a lot of fun to play with."

Grandpa:
"Grandma is allergic to cats. It's probably for the best. I doubt the kittens would like you as much as you like them."

Remi:
"Grandpa, everyone tells me that I'm adorable. I don't understand why the cats don't think so."

Grandpa:
Just shakes his head and grins.

Remi:

"Grandpa, why do they always scatter and hide when I go over to their house to play? At first, I thought they were playing hide and seek, but they never come out. If I even get close to their house, they have a hissy fit."

Grandpa:

"You tend to have that effect on cats."

Remi:

"You should talk to them Grandpa and tell them to be better neighbors."

Grandpa:

"I tried to, Remi. But once they saw me with you my reputation was ruined."

Remi just wouldn't let this go:

Remi:

"Grandpa, you need to be more convincing. We both like to chase birds. Tell them I can chase them up the tree and they can take it from there."

Grandpa:

"Okay, Remi. I'll try one more time to convince them to play with you. But don't get your hopes up. I think their minds are made up."

This look says it all...

Artwork by OpenClipart-Vectors, Pixabay.com

Left: Louise, English Angora
Right: Loaf, Newfound Dwarf

Louise and Loaf

These two rodents are our son, Matt's, roommates. If ever there were two bunnies who were well cared for and spoiled rotten, it's Louise and Loaf. Loaf is the mild-mannered one. Louise is a bit territorial and lets everyone know why Thumper was given his name in the cartoon. She's an adorably different looking rabbit.

One day, Remi shared her thoughts on what she assumed were just house guests for the weekend:

Remi:
"Grandpa, the bunnies are quieter than a house mouse."

"I always have to sneak up on them. Then they make this thumping noise with their back feet. I've heard you say you're going to put your foot down with me, but now the rabbits are doing it too. And they mean it."

Grandpa:
"The reasons are very different, Remi. When I say it, I mean that I am going to be stricter with you. When the rabbits do it, they're telling you to stay back."

Remi:
"I think I like it better when you put your foot down Grandpa. I can ignore that."

Grandpa:
"As usual, I think the point went over your head."

Remi:
"Grandpa, I usually get the message when it comes with a treat. I particularly like the salmon-flavored ones."

Eating habits always seem to be of interest to Remi:

Remi:
"Grandpa, Matthew sure does feed those rabbits a lot of lettuce. Do they ever eat meat?"

Grandpa:
"I'm sure if you get too close, they might try to."

Grandpa was picking on Remi one day when they were playing fetch. And as is usually the case, Grandpa was doing the fetching.

Grandpa:
"You little, hair-brain twit."

Remi:
"Stop calling me that, Grandpa. I'm not a rabbit."

Remi is always looking for a new playmate:

Remi:
"Grandpa, you never let me play with the bunnies' downstairs."

"They smell funny, but they love to hop all over the place. I can do that too."

Grandpa:
"Remi, we've talked about this. The last time we let you loose to play with Louise it looked like you both bolted out of the starting gate at the Kentucky Derby. You were both neck-and-neck, but you were the only one who was having any fun. It's best if someone holds you and you just sniff them."

One day Remi was watching (from a distance) the rabbits play together in the grass. She had some thoughts:

Remi:
"Grandpa, Louise looks like a cartoon character. Where did she get those ears?"

Grandpa:
"Remi, it's not nice to make fun of other critters. Louise is a special, adorable little rodent, just like you."

Remi:
"I am not a rodent, Grandpa!"

Grandpa:
"You're right, Remi. I'm sorry for calling you a rodent. But you do get a little squirrelly sometimes."

Remi:
"That reminds me. I think one of them is still hiding up in the tree. I better go check."

When someone in the house gets special treatment, Remi tends to notice:

Remi:
"Grandpa, why do the bunnies get to go potty inside?"

Grandpa:
"Bunnies go potty a lot, Remi. That's why they have a corner to go potty in."

Remi:
"If I go a lot, can I go in a corner instead of going outside?"

Grandpa:
"I'm sorry, Remi. But the rules are different for the rabbits."

Remi:
"That's not fair, Grandpa. They get treated special."

Grandpa:
"Life's not fair, Remi. It's just reasonable."

Remi mutters to herself:
"We'll see about that. I have just the corner in mind."

Just a random thought... It's a good thing Louise and Loaf are fixed. Or someone would have to move out. And it isn't Remi or Grandpa.

Artwork by Jo Justino, Pixabay.com

Artwork by Dmitry Abramov, Pixabay.com

On her many walks around the neighborhood, Remi is always taking notes:

Remi:
"Grandpa, why is it okay for you to shout 'hi' to people on the street but I have to be quiet when I see a puppy?"

Grandpa:
"Well, I usually just say 'hi' once, wave, and keep on walking. You say 'hi' more than once and stop and visit everyone for several minutes. I'm not getting any younger. And all that your friends want to do is lick and sniff."

Remi:
"Grandpa, that's what some of the kids at the high school are doing when we go by there for walks. I think I behave pretty good, all things considered."

Grandpa:
"You do have a point. Next time, feel free to bark at them. They could use a breather."

Remi:
"I just love the walks that you, Grandma, and Caleb take me on, Grandpa."

Grandpa:
"What do you like the most about your walks, Remi?"

Remi:
"I get to lead the way. All the grass, and smells. And all the friends I see. I know where they all live too. I never forget something like that, Grandpa."

Grandpa:
"If only your memory was that good about everything."

Remi:
"Grandpa, word on the sidewalk is that more and more houses are adding puppies. This would be a good time to invest in kennel futures."

Grandpa:
"Is that a reliable source, Remi?"

Remi:
"It's coming from inside, Grandpa."

That got Remi to thinking:

Remi:
"Grandpa, you would never trade me for someone would you?"

Grandpa:
"Trade? No. Sell, maybe. You keep telling me that you're priceless."

Remi:
"Yes. I do have that going for me."

Artwork by Sabrina, Pixabay.com

It hasn't gone unnoticed by Remi that she isn't on the top of the food chain. That doesn't always sit well with her:

Remi:
"Grandpa, why don't I get to have a seat at the table and eat your food? It smells so much better than that crunchy stuff you put in my bowl. It's so dry. I never get to sit up at the table. I'm lucky if I ever get scraps."

Grandpa:
"Remi, the dinner table is just for humans."

Remi:
"I still think you could share a little more. I'll share my food with you."

Grandpa:
"Hard pass on that one, Remi."

Remi:

"Grandpa, why doesn't Grandma give me scraps from her eating bowl like you do?"

Grandpa:

"Shhh. Don't let Grandma know. It's our little secret."

Remi:

"Your secrets' not safe with me Grandpa. I love table scraps. You're not supposed to keep secrets from Grandma. Especially this one."

Artwork by AnnaliseArt, Pixabay.com

Remi really likes to go for rides in the car. That got her to thinking:

Remi:
"Grandpa, why can't I drive?

Grandpa:
"Well, Remi. I would let you take the wheel but at the first sight of one of your friends we'd either be on the sidewalk, in the ditch, or on someone's front yard. Let's stick with you barking orders from the front seat."

Remi:
"I'm not the one barking orders from the front seat, Grandpa. That's Grandma. I just bark at friends that are out for a walk. You should talk to Grandma about this."

Grandpa:
"I think it's best if we just keep this conversation between us. Let sleeping dogs lie, so to speak."

Remi:
"What?"

Grandpa:
"Never mind."

One day we were doing a lot of driving around to pick up things here and there. Remi was getting concerned when the gas gauge was moving closer to empty:

Remi:
"Grandpa, what will we do if we run out of gas?"

Grandpa:
"You're going to have to get out and push."

Remi:
"Grandpa, I'm too little. My cousin Bella can pull us though. Those Siberian Huskies really know how to mush."

Remi always seems to notice when one of her relatives does something that she has never seen before:

Remi:
"Grandpa, why can't I stick my head out the window like other puppies do? It looks like a lot of fun."

Grandpa:
"It's not safe for little puppies to have their head out the window."

Remi:
"But other puppies get to do it."

Grandpa:
"Well, maybe we can have someone hold you and you can try it. Maybe after you have just had a bath we could go for a ride. It would dry your ears faster."

Remi:
"I don't think so, Grandpa. I don't like baths."

One day Grandpa and Remi were out for a drive. Remi must have missed a meal:

Remi:
"Grandpa, if you don't have any plans right now, can we drive up to the little window at Culver's so I can get a pup cup? They're free you know. They're my favorite."

Grandpa:
"Anything with the word "pup" in it is your favorite, Remi."

Remi:
"Was that a Yes, Grandpa?"

Remi is never shy about letting Grandpa know what she's thinking:

Remi:
"Grandpa, you're not a very good driver. I can see those cars coming from a mile away. And you can't see that car right in front of us. Are you supposed to smash into each other? You should honk your horn more. It sure works for me to get someone's attention."

Grandpa:
"You have a lot of advice for someone who has never been behind the wheel."

Remi:
"Yes, I have Grandpa. Just before we left our house, I stopped to leave my mark. So did Buddy."

Artwork by Chris Gorgio

Remi's second-to-the-least-favorite thing to do is to have a bath. It's always a drama. A mud puddle is always welcome. A clean spray of water? Not so much.

Remi:
"Grandpa, why do I need to have a bath? I like my smell. Don't you?"

Grandpa:
"Having a bath once a month, or after you roll around in a pile of something, is good for your coat."

Remi:
"But Grandpa, I don't wear a coat."

Grandpa:
"I mean your fur coat."

Remi:
"Oh. Why don't the rabbits have to take a bath, Grandpa? Is it because they'll hop out of the tub?"

Grandpa:
"I can see why you would think that Remi. But rabbits don't need baths.
They groom themselves and rabbits groom each other. It's a sign of
respect when one rabbit grooms another rabbit *(according to our son,
Matt).*"

Remi:
"I can groom myself, Grandpa. That way you won't have to change
clothes after my bath is done."

Grandpa:
"Let's just stick with bath time."

Remi:
"Does Grandma groom you, Grandpa?

Grandpa:
"More than you know, Remi. More than you know."

Artwork by OpenClipArt-Vectors, Pixabay.com

Having her nails done.

Remi's least favorite thing to do is have her nails cut and filed.

When you haven't made it to the groomer and company is coming, sometimes you need to trim the nails to prevent unnecessary scratches and snags in clothes when greeting guests at the door.

It's also Caleb and Grandpa's least favorite thing to do. That wild look in Remi's eyes can be seen in ours as well.

Grandpa:
"Remi, it's time to trim your nails. Let's go outside and sit in the grass and have some treats."

Remi:
"That worked the first time, Grandpa."

Haircut

Remi is a year and half and has yet to have a haircut with a groomer. Just the nails. All she has needed is a trim here and there to look presentable for her special friend, Buddy, next door.

She wants to look good for Brewer too, but he's older and keeps a watchful eye on Remi and Buddy.

But it hasn't gone unnoticed that Grandpa does need a haircut once and awhile:

Remi:
"Grandpa, isn't your hair supposed to look fuller after you go to the groomer? I've noticed that I can see through your coat on top. Did the clippers get too close?"

Grandpa:
"I don't want to talk about it, Remi."

Artwork by ArtRose, Pixabay.com

The neighbors' next door have a miniature schnauzer named Buddy. Remi and Buddy have become very good friends. When one of them goes outside they look for the other one and usually call out to see if they get a response. One day, Remi hit me with the conversation I was dreading.

Remi:
"Grandpa, I sure like that cute little puppy next door. They call him Buddy. He's almost 2 years older than me. I know that you and Grandma have talked about girls dating older boys. Is he too old for me? Is it okay if I play with him?"

Grandpa:
"Sure, Remi. You can play with Buddy any time you like."

Remi:
"It would be a lot less trouble for you and Grandma if Buddy just moved in with us. He can share Caleb's and my room."

Grandpa:
"Do you remember those cold days that come around when the ground is white?"

Remi:
"Burr. Yup. Those are ruff."

Grandpa:
"Well, it will be one of those days before Buddy moves in!"

After thinking it over for a bit, Remi tried a new approach:

Remi:
"Grandpa, when do I get to have a sleepover with my friend Buddy?"

Grandpa:
"You need to talk to Grandma about that."

Remi:
"Grandpa, sometimes when I jump up on your bed there's no room for me to lay down between you and Grandma. I need to tell my friend Buddy that we should try that."

Grandpa:
"Grandma is really hot, so I like to stay close."

Remi:
"Oh. Buddy was telling me we could be friends with benefits."

Grandpa:
"Remi, have you been in Buddy's kennel?"

Remi:
"No, Grandpa, that's his house."

Grandpa:
"Good. That's one doorway you cannot cross."

Artwork by Christophe Gorkhs, Pixabay.com

While Remi is Caleb's puppy, Grandpa can't help but spoil her rotten. How can anyone stay mad at something that cute?

The joy a puppy brings to a human, especially Remi, is a multiple-times-a-day, daily occurrence with her. She has brought so much happiness and joy to our son, Caleb. A near-constant snuggle buddy, Remi loves to cuddle up next to you and chill. Naps or not, she loves to snuggle.

Sometimes it can get a little too close. One night when Grandma and Caleb were away for the night, Remi got to sleep with Grandpa. She started out in the middle of the bed. Grandpa's head was on the pillow and exhausted. Five minutes later, Remi had her head on Grandma's pillow. Five minutes later, and her head was between the pillows. Five minutes later, her head was on the corner of Grandpa's pillow, touching his head. Another five minutes later, and her nose was right under Grandpa's nose and breathing into his nostrils.

That was the last move. Remi was placed up to Grandpa's chest and reminded where her kennel was. She slept like a rock. Grandpa did not.

In the morning, Grandpa rose from the soft comfort of the bed and smiled. Dogs really are Grandpa's best friend.

Remi - 2 months old

After reading this, you may be thinking to yourself that this guy needs a life or a wife.

Well, I happily have both.

Although, I can get by with saying some things to Remi that I can't otherwise say to my usually understanding wife.

Paws Up!

Artwork by Clker, Pixabay.com

Cooper was the first puppy the family welcomed into our home. She was a cock-a-poo that weighed 12 pounds at her maximum. Spoiled rotten and the most lovable little creature you could ever hold. Resting in peace in the puppy playground above.

December 24, 2005 – May 14, 2017

Thank You!

Artwork by OpenClipart-Vectors, Pixabay.com

Thank you for reading this book.

I hope it tickled your funny bones at least a little bit.